Contents

Tables

<Page intentionally left blank>

Executive Summary

The travel and tourism industry plays an important role in achieving the National Export Initiative goal of doubling exports by the end of 2014. In fact, the President's Export Council and the President's Jobs and Competitiveness Council both highlight the benefits of this sector and make recommendations to increase the number of visitors to the United States. Furthermore, the President on January 19, 2012, signed Executive Order 13597, *Establishing Visa and Foreign Visitor Processing Goals and the Task Force On Travel Competitiveness.*

In 2011, 63 million international visitors to the United States accounted for a total of $153 billion in travel and tourism exports, 25 percent of total U.S. services exports. These expenditures are one of the largest categories of U.S. services exports with leisure travelers being the largest consumers of travel services. Visitors to the United States fall into two categories: those that need a visa to enter and those that do not. Over the past 10 years, travel expenditures of visitors who need a visa to enter the United States have increased by 13 percent. According to the 2009 Survey of International Air Travelers, the average duration of leisure trips for visitors to the United States who need a visa is nearly five nights longer that for visa-free visitors. In this brief, we assess the contribution of overseas leisure travelers (except those from Canada and Mexico by land) that need a visa to enter the United States because this group can play an important role in growing exports in U.S. travel services.

Based on the 2009 Survey of International Air Travelers, we find:

- The expenditure share of all overseas travelers who need a visa to enter the United States is 47 percent, with most of that share coming from leisure travelers.

- If the number of overseas leisure travelers that require a visa could be increased by 10 percent, aggregate leisure expenditures would be increased by 4.6 percent or by $1.25 billion.

- For the National Export Initiative priority countries Brazil, China, and India, a 10 percent increase in leisure visitors would increase travel expenditures by $344 million.

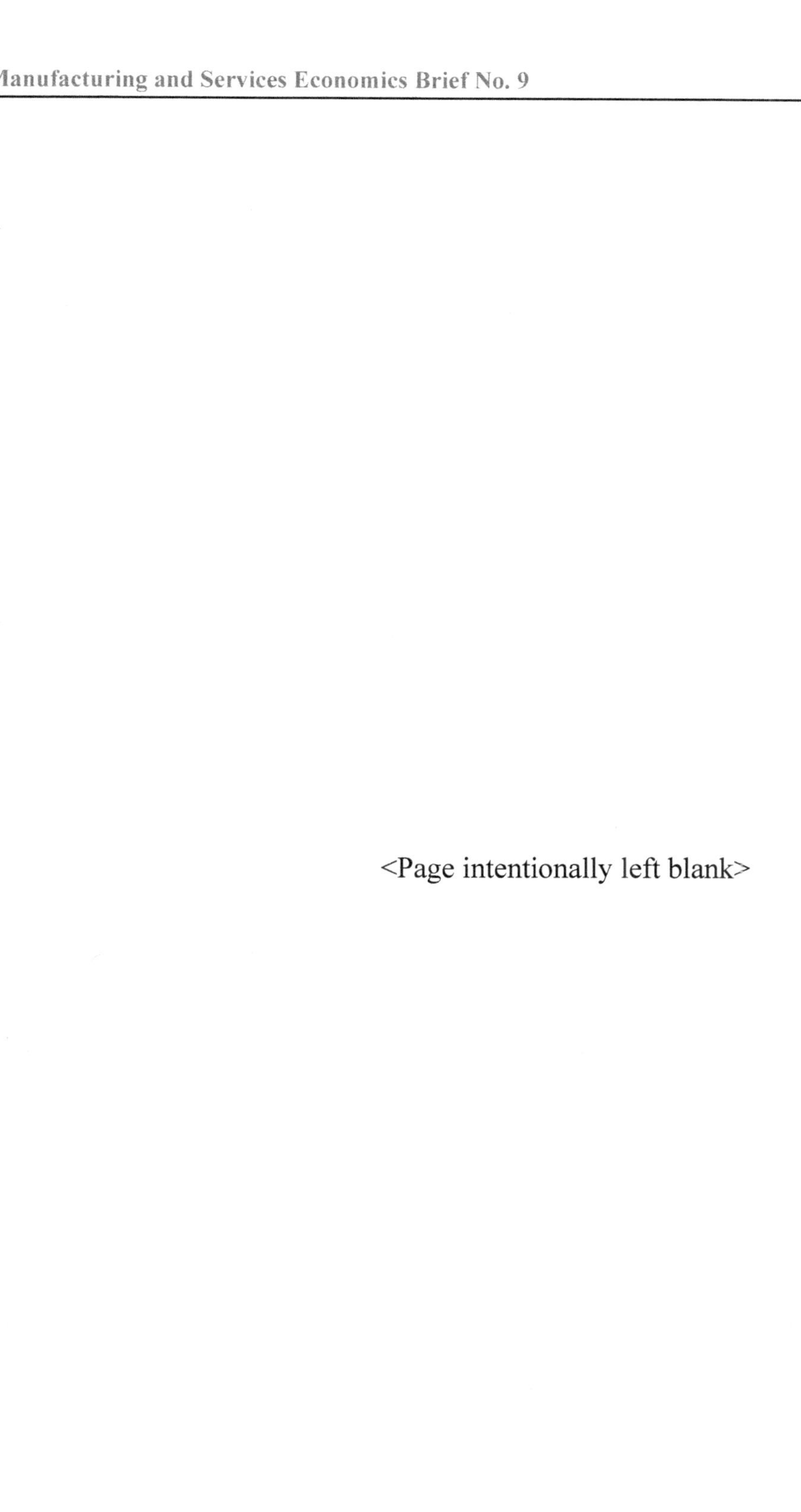

<Page intentionally left blank>

1. Introduction

Despite the recent global recession, international travel flows have remained high. According to the United Nations World Tourism Organization, there were a total of 880 million world-wide travelers in 2009, and 940 million in 2010. Within the Americas, the United States remains the top destination. Globally, the United States has been the second most popular destination for the past two years. Nevertheless, there is significant room to grow exports in travel services by increasing the U.S. share of international travelers.

The travel and tourism industry plays an important role in achieving the National Export Initiative goal of doubling exports by the end of 2014. In fact, the President's Export Council and the President's Jobs and Competitiveness Council both highlight the benefits of this sector and make recommendations to increase the number of visitors to the United States. Furthermore, the President on January 19, 2012, signed Executive Order 13597, *Establishing Visa and Foreign Visitor Processing Goals and the Task Force On Travel Competitiveness.*[1]

In 2011, 63 million international visitors to the United States accounted for a total of $153 billion in travel and tourism exports, or 25 percent of total U.S. services exports.[2] Spending in the U.S. (travel receipts) totaled $116 billion and passenger fare receipts (spending on U.S. carriers) were $37 billion. Overseas travelers (excluding Canadians and Mexicans by land) to the United States totaled 27.9 million visitors who spent a total of $120 billion, $90 billion of which was for travel receipts and $30 billion on airfare receipts. These expenditures are one of the largest categories of U.S. services exports with leisure travelers being the largest consumers of travel services.

Visitors to the United States fall into two categories: those that need a visa to enter and those that do not. Over the past 10 years, travel expenditures of visitors who need a visa to enter the United States have increased by 13 percent. According to the 2009 Survey of International Air Travelers (SIAT), the average duration of leisure trips for visitors to the United States who need a visa is nearly five nights longer that for visa-free visitors. In this brief, we assess the

---

[1] Federal Register, Vol. 77, No. 15, January 24, 2012, pp. 3373-75.

[2] Office of Travel and Tourism Industries, *International Visitation to the United States: A Statistical Summary of U.S. Visitation (2011)* (Washington, DC: U.S. Department of Commerce, International Trade Administration, 2011).

contribution of overseas leisure travelers (except those from Canada and Mexico by land) that need a visa to enter the United States because this group can play an important role in growing exports in U.S. travel services.

For calculating travel expenditures it is necessary to carefully account for shares of visa-required and visa-free travelers. For example, some residents of non-Visa Waiver Program (VWP) countries hold passports from VWP countries and can travel to the United States visa-free. The Department of Homeland Security (DHS) regulates the Visa Waiver Program, a program under which citizens from participating countries do not require visas for short-term (90 day) leisure travel to the United States.[3] Currently, 36 countries participate in the VWP, and most of the participating countries are developed market economies.[4] While only 20 percent of the countries represented by visitors to the United States are VWP counties, they account for 40 percent of all non-Canadian arrivals. This implies that 60 percent of non-Canadian international travelers require a visa to enter to the United States.[5]

We use individual responses by overseas travelers from the Survey of International Air Travelers in 2009 to identify visa-required travelers and examine growth in U.S. travel service exports for leisure travelers. We do this in three steps. First, we calculate the fraction of visa-required business and leisure travelers from each country, based on their country of citizenship (regardless of whether the individual has already been issued a visa or needs a new issuance).[6] Second, we use this fraction to calculate separate dollar amounts of travel expenditures by visa-required travelers from each country of residence and total dollar amounts of travel expenditures

---

[3]Legislation created the VWP in 1986 as a pilot program; subsequent legislation in 2000 modified many of its requirements and made it a permanent program.

[4] See Appendix A for a list of all VWP countries.

[5] Many travelers from VWP countries still require a visa because they are residents, but not citizens, of those countries. As long as a citizen of a VWP country meets eligibility requirement, including that the business or leisure visit not exceed 90 days, the traveler may enter the United States without a visa. The VWP eligibility guidelines still require that a resident of the VWP country obtain a visa if he or she is not a citizen of that country. For example, if an Australian resident is an Algerian citizen, he or she must have a visa to enter the United States. In addition, regardless of citizenship status, all non-American and non-Canadian travelers require a visa if the duration of their stay exceeds 90 days, or the purpose of travel is not tourism or temporary business. See Appendix B for VWP detailed eligibility requirements that are specified by law.

[6] Visas are generally issued for multiple trips and can be valid for years. Around 11 percent of international arrivals use a visa obtained within the same year as the trip. This analysis includes repeat visitors who have multi-year visas. For example, visas that are issued for non-immigrant travelers from Brazil are valid for 10 years.

for all countries by the purpose of the visit. Finally, we use the actual expenditures of visa-required leisure travelers to calculate the increase in exports of U.S. travel services resulting from a 10 percent increase of these travelers.[7] This calculation provides an estimate of the *potential* growth of U.S. travel and tourism exports because we do not directly observe the expenditures of additional visa-required travelers.

2. Share of U.S. Services Exports to Nonresident Air Travelers Who Require a Visa

2.1. Data on Inbound Overseas International Travel

We focus on the expenditures of nonresident air travelers who visited the United States in 2009, because we have detailed information about this group from individual responses to the Survey of International Air Travelers (SIAT). The SIAT is a primary research program that gathers statistical data about air passenger travelers to and from the United States. It is used to calculate aggregate arrivals and travel expenditure values by each country to construct official government statistics on travel and tourism trends. The U.S. Department of Commerce estimates that air travelers accounted for 57.1 percent of all nonresident arrivals in 2009 and 68.3 percent of all non-Canadian, nonresident arrivals.[8]

A unique feature of the individual-level records from this survey is that each air traveler is asked to separately state his or her country of residence and citizenship.[9] The SIAT files, to be consistent with the U.S. Department of Homeland Security's I-94 data, provide a weight for each respondent.[10] The survey responses of the visitors who do not reside in the United States are weighted to match the aggregated I-94 arrival records to adjust for over- and under sampling in

[7] 10 percent is the growth rate in volume of international travelers between 2009 and 2010.

[8] Office of Travel and Tourism Industries, *International Visitation to the United States: A Statistical Summary of U.S. Arrivals (2009).*

[9] Non-citizens are required to do so also on the DHS I-94/W, ESTA.

[10] I-94 is a form denoting the *Arrival-Departure Record* of particular foreigners used by U.S. Customs and Border Protection. Form I-94 must be completed at the time of entry to the United States by foreign citizens that are being admitted into the United States in a nonimmigrant visa status.

the SIAT.[11] Although the matching is based on an individual's country of residence, the weighted SIAT data can also be used to calculate aggregate arrivals by country of citizenship.

2.2. Share of All Visa-Required Air Travelers

The SIAT dataset does not indicate whether individual respondents required visas. However, we observe the respondent's country of citizenship (as well as his or her country of residence), and with this information, we can infer which air travelers required a visa.[12] We classify each traveler in the 2009 SIAT as either requiring or not requiring a visa. Travelers who did not require a visa are either citizens of the United States or Canada, or citizens of countries that participate in the VWP and stay fewer than 90 days.[13] Note that this implies that residents of non-VWP countries that have VWP citizenship are assumed to travel visa-free (and that residents of VWP countries who have non-VWP citizenship must have a visa).

In our analysis, we consider two groups of nonresident air travelers: business and leisure. These two groups accounted for 95 percent of all nonresident air travelers. The business group includes nonresident air travelers who reported that the main purpose of their trip was business/ professional, or convention/conference/trade show. The leisure group includes nonresident air travelers who reported that their main purpose was leisure, recreation, holidays, sightseeing, or visiting friends or relatives. Table 1 reports the fraction of all nonresident arrivals by purpose of travel.

We present these fractions for the top 25 countries in each VWP category (participant or nonparticipant). The average share of leisure travelers from VWP countries (74 percent) is higher than the share from non-VWP countries (67 percent). For example, by comparing the top five countries by total arrivals from each category, we observe that 78 percent of German travelers were leisure travelers as compared to 47 percent Indian travelers. The patterns are similar for

[11] The weights in the SIAT data are constructed by CIC Research Inc. For convenience, we provide the details on how CIC constructs the weights in Appendix D.

[12] However, some travelers from VWP countries still choose to travel to the United States on a visa. For example, a visitor may want to extend his/her stay in the United States beyond the 90 days allowed under the VWP. Since the number of travelers who stay longer than 90 days is small, for purposes of this analysis, we assume all travelers with VWP passports visit the United States visa-free.

[13] An eligible traveler under the VWP must meet many additional requirements. In the SIAT data, we observe only the duration of stay of each responding traveler.

other countries. Interestingly, the average share of business travelers from VWP is 26 percent, compared to 33 percent from non-VWP countries.

Table 1 - Fractions and Counts of Arrivals by Purpose Type and Visa Program in 2009

	VWP				Non-VWP		
Country	**Business**	**Leisure**	**Total**	**Country**	**Business**	**Leisure**	**Total**
United Kingdom	0.19	0.81	3,678,847	Mexico (air)	0.32	0.68	1,511,181
Japan	0.14	0.86	2,843,800	Brazil	0.23	0.77	871,721
Germany	0.22	0.78	1,574,905	India	0.53	0.47	498,780
France	0.18	0.82	1,083,456	Venezuela	0.12	0.88	491,504
Italy	0.22	0.78	716,327	China	0.56	0.44	473,266
South Korea	0.33	0.67	668,027	Colombia	0.23	0.77	409,582
Australia	0.17	0.83	654,053	Argentina	0.22	0.78	346,476
Spain	0.15	0.85	564,107	Israel	0.29	0.71	291,666
Netherlands	0.23	0.77	510,758	Taiwan	0.46	0.54	224,361
Ireland	0.16	0.84	397,396	Dominican Rep.	0.58	0.42	216,944
Switzerland	0.27	0.73	332,838	Bahamas	0.26	0.74	194,613
Sweden	0.26	0.74	314,884	Guatemala	0.27	0.73	182,216
Denmark	0.23	0.77	235,688	Jamaica	0.26	0.74	176,734
Belgium	0.31	0.69	233,499	Ecuador	0.21	0.79	163,964
Norway	0.27	0.73	186,811	Peru	0.16	0.84	154,649
Austria	0.23	0.77	151,541	Costa Rica	0.53	0.47	154,528
New Zealand	0.34	0.66	114,685	Philippines	0.29	0.71	151,375
Finland	0.25	0.75	109,114	Russia	0.34	0.66	140,189
Singapore	0.53	0.47	101,017	Trinidad	0.27	0.73	134,082
Portugal	0.29	0.71	67,107	Chile	0.51	0.49	122,197
Czech Republic	0.43	0.57	60,829	El Salvador	0.50	0.50	120,077
Greece	0.22	0.78	54,505	Honduras	0.23	0.77	112,616
Hungary	0.20	0.80	45,374	Poland	0.19	0.81	109,468
Iceland	0.30	0.70	27,714	Panama	0.44	0.56	107,651
Slovenia	0.29	0.71	17,726	Hong Kong	0.32	0.68	106,641
Average	**0.26**	**0.74**			**0.33**	**0.67**	

Note: Totals reported are a sum of business and leisure travelers for the respective countries.
Source: Authors' calculations.

Next, we estimate the shares of nonresident business and leisure travelers who require visas. To calculate this estimate, we divide the counts of visa-required travelers by the sum of counts of visa-required and visa-free travelers in the group. These estimates are presented in Table 2.

Table 2 - Total Counts of Visa-Required and Visa-Free Overseas Arrivals by Travel Purpose in 2009

155 Countries	Business		Leisure	
	No Visa	Visa	No Visa	Visa
Total	3,139,373	2,799,972	12,254,571	5,652,816
Visa share	47 percent		32 percent	
Visa share total	35 percent			

Source: Authors' calculations.

In 2009, 47 percent of all nonresident business air travelers required visas. For nonresident leisure air travelers, 32 percent required visas. While the total share of visa-required travelers is 35 percent, this share varies significantly depending on the country of residence, whether the country participates in the VWP, and whether the travelers were American citizens. For example, the total share of visa-required travelers from Brazil, China and India exceeded 90 percent.

2.3. Share of U.S. Travel Services Exports to All Visa-Required Nonresident Air Travelers

Our next step is to compute the dollar value and shares of travel expenditures by visa-required travelers. To obtain the dollar value of travel expenditures, we follow the methodology of calculating annual travel receipts implemented by the Bureau of Economic Analysis (BEA).[14] First, we calculate average travel expenditures in the United States per air traveler by country of residence and by purpose of visit. Next, we multiply these travel expenditures by I-94 counts of travelers by country that are reported by DHS. Finally, we calculate the share of total expenditures from nonresident overseas air travelers in each group who require visas by using our estimate of the share of travelers who required a visa and the per capita expenditures within each group. Overall, the expenditure share for visitors (excluding Canada) that need a visa is 47 percent. For business travelers who need a visa it is 51 percent, and for leisure travelers who need a visa it is 46 percent.[15] These estimates are presented in Table 3.

[14] BEA reports total travel receipts regardless of purpose of travel and visa requirements.

[15] See Appendix C for a robustness check that compares the travel expenditure calculations that are based on SIAT with travel receipts statistics from BEA.

Table 3 - Total Expenditures of Visa-Required and Visa-Free Overseas Arrivals by Travel Type in 2009

155 Countries	Business		Leisure	
	No Visa	Visa	No Visa	Visa
Total	$4,216,670,505	$4,425,400,205	$31,285,051,243	$26,606,541,239
Shares	49 percent	51 percent	54 percent	46 percent
Visa share total	47 percent			

Source: Authors' calculations.

3. Implications of the Estimates

We use the expenditure shares to calculate the change in U.S. travel services exports if the number of visa-required travelers increased. There is a basic mathematical relationship between the growth rate in overall U.S. travel and tourism exports to nonresident air travelers and the growth rate of each of the components. The growth rate of total exports is a share weighted average of the growth rates of the components:

$$\%\Delta Total\ Exports = \sum (Share\ of\ Component\ \times \%\Delta Component\ Exports)$$

We find that a substantial fraction of air travelers who visited the United States in 2009 required a visa. When we separate the air travelers by the main purpose of their visit, 47 percent of business and 32 percent of leisure travelers required a visa. Using the same data, we find that 47 percent of all travel *expenditures* come from visa-required air travelers, with most of that share coming from leisure travelers. An increase in the number of these travelers can potentially increase total travel and tourism exports in proportion to the expenditure shares.[16] During 2010, the growth rate in total number of leisure travelers was 10 percent. Using that rate as an illustration and applying the above formula, we find that increasing overseas leisure travelers that require a visa by 10 percent would increase aggregate leisure travel expenditures by 4.6 percent or by $1.25 billion.

[16] An increase in travel expenditure can come from a larger volume of travelers or from an increase in spending on travel services by existing travelers. We do not distinguish between the alternatives in this brief.

We apply the formula to quantify the change in exports in travel services for air travelers for the NEI priority countries of Brazil, China, and India. Over 90 percent of travelers from those countries are required to obtain a visa to enter the United States. We estimate that leisure visitors from Brazil, China and India spent nearly $2.4 billon, $796 million and $655 million, respectively, on U.S. travel services. We find that increasing leisure travelers by 10 percent would increase the aggregate travel and tourism expenditures for Brazil, China, and India by $213 million, $72 million, and $59 million, respectively, or by a total of $344 million.

4. Conclusion

Using individual-level data from the SIAT, this brief calculates the fraction of air travelers who need a visa to enter the United States and the benefits of expanding the number of these travelers. It is not possible to predict the dollar costs of expanding visa services to accommodate this potential increase in demand without specifying the details of the changes. However, it is straightforward to determine what share of current U.S. travel and tourism exports are linked to visa-required visitors and thereby gauge the potential benefits in the form of increased U.S. services exports, which we estimate could be over $1 billion. We also find that U.S. services exports can benefit significantly from an increase volume of travelers from the three NEI priority countries of Brazil, China and India, which we estimate could be over $300 million.

The large share of expenditures on travel services by visa-required travelers suggests that an increase in the number of such travelers has the potential to significantly increase U.S. services exports and, in the process, significantly boost the U.S. travel industry. This could be achieved through encouraging holders of multi-year visas to make repeat trips and expanding the number of first-time visitors, or a combination of these factors.

Appendix A. List of Countries and VWP Participation in 2009

Country of Residence	VWP	Country of Residence	VWP
Afghanistan	no	Ethiopia	no
Albania	no	**Finland**	**yes**
Algeria	no	Fr.Polynesia	no
Andorra	**yes**	**France**	**yes**
Angola	no	French Guiana	no
Anguilla	no	Gabon	no
Antigua & Barbuda	no	Gambia	no
Argentina	no	Georgia	no
Armenia	no	**Germany**	**yes**
Aruba	no	Ghana	no
Australia	**yes**	Gibraltar	no
Austria	**yes**	**Greece**	**yes**
Azerbaijan	no	Grenada	no
Bahamas	no	Guadeloupe	no
Bahrain	no	Guatemala	no
Bangladesh	no	Guinea	no
Barbados	no	Guyana	no
Belarus	no	Haiti	no
Belgium	**yes**	Honduras	no
Belize	no	Hong Kong	no
Benin	no	**Hungary**	**yes**
Bermuda	no	**Iceland**	**yes**
Bolivia	no	India	no
Bosnia/Herzegovina	no	Indonesia	no
Botswana	no	Iran	no
Brazil	no	Iraq	no
Brit Virgin Is.	no	**Ireland**	**yes**
Brunei	**yes**	Israel	no
Bulgaria	no	**Italy**	**yes**
Burma/Myanmar	no	Ivory Coast	no
Burundi	no	Jamaica	no
Cameroon	no	**Japan**	**yes**
Cayman Is.	no	Jordan	no
Chad	no	Kampuchea/Cambodia	no
Chile	no	Kazakhstan	no
China, Peoples Rep.	no	Kenya	no
Colombia	no	**Korea, South**	**yes**
Congo	no	Kyrgyzstan	no
Cook Is.	no	Kuwait	no
Costa Rica	no	Laos	no
Croatia	no	**Latvia**	**yes**
Curacao	no	Lebanon	no
Cyprus	no	Lesotho	no
Czech Republic	**yes**	Liberia	no
Denmark	**yes**	**Lichtenstein**	**yes**
Dominica	no	**Lithuania**	**yes**
Dominican Rep	no	**Luxembourg**	**yes**
Ecuador	no	Macao/Macau	no
Egypt	no	Macedonia	no
El Salvador	no	Malawi	no
Equatorial Guinea	no	Malaysia	no
Estonia	**yes**	Maldives	no

Country of Residence	VWP	Country of Residence	VWP
Malta	**yes**	Sri Lanka	no
Mauritania	no	St Eustatius/Statia	no
Mexico	no	St Kitts	no
Moldova	no	St Lucia	no
Monaco	**yes**	St Martin	no
Mongolia	no	St Vincent	no
Montenegro	no	Sudan	no
Morocco	no	Suriname	no
Mozambique	no	Swaziland	no
Namibia	no	**Sweden**	**yes**
Nepal	no	**Switzerland**	**yes**
Netherlands	**yes**	Syria	no
Netherlands Antilles	no	Taiwan	no
Nevis	no	Tajikistan	no
New Zealand	**yes**	Tanzania	no
Nicaragua	no	Thailand	no
Niger	no	Togo	no
Nigeria	no	Tonga	no
Norway	**yes**	Trinidad & Tobago	no
Okinawa/Ryukyu Is.	no	Tunisia	no
Oman	no	Turkey	no
Pakistan	no	Turks & Caicos	no
Palau	no	Uganda	no
Panama	no	Ukraine	no
Paraguay	no	UAE	no
Peru	no	**United Kingdom**	**yes**
Philippines	no	Burkina Faso	no
Poland	no	Uruguay	no
Portugal	**yes**	Uzbekistan	no
Qatar	no	Venezuela	no
Reunion Is.	no	Vietnam	no
Romania	no	Western Samoa	no
Russia	no	Yemen	no
Rwanda	no	Zaire	no
San Marino	**yes**	Zambia	no
Rwanda	no	Zimbabwe	no
San Marino	**yes**		
Saudi Arabia	no		
Senegal	no		
Serbia	no		
Sierra Leone	no		
Singapore	**yes**		
Slovakia	**yes**		
Slovenia	**yes**		
Somalia	no		
South Africa	no		
Spain	**yes**		

Source: U.S. Department State

Appendix B. Visa Waiver Program Eligibility Requirements

By law, travelers seeking to enter the United States under the VWP must meet the following requirements, provided that the travelers are citizens of VWP countries:[17]

- Travelers have received an authorization to travel under the VWP through the Electronic System for Travel Authorization.
- They present the appropriate type of passport valid for six months past their expected stay in the United States (unless country-specific agreements provide exemptions). This requirement is in addition to other passport requirements for all categories of passports—regular, diplomatic, and official—when travelers are seeking to enter the United States for business or tourist purposes for a maximum of 90 days.
- The purpose of their stay in the United States is leisure (WT) or business (visitor [WB] visa) for 90 days or fewer of travel. (If in doubt, travelers should check with the nearest U.S. embassy or consulate to verify that what they plan to do is considered leisure or business.) Transit through the United States is generally permitted.
- Foreign media representatives planning to engage in that vocation in the United States are not eligible for VWP travel because the purpose of their stay does not qualify as *business*. These professionals must obtain a nonimmigrant media (I) visa. Travelers planning to work or study cannot travel on the VWP, and they must obtain the appropriate visa to travel to the United States.
- If arriving by air or sea, travelers are traveling on an approved carrier and have a return trip ticket to any foreign destination.
- They can demonstrate the intent to stay 90 days or fewer in the United States and have sufficient funds to support themselves while in the United States.
- VWP travelers who have been admitted under the VWP and who make a short trip to Canada, Mexico, or an adjacent island generally can be readmitted to the United States under the VWP for the balance of their original admission period.

[17] The U.S. Department of State, "Visa Waiver Program," *http://travel.state.gov/visa/temp/without/without_1990.html.*

<Page intentionally left blank>

Appendix C. Robustness of Travel Expenditure Calculations

We checked the robustness of our travel expenditure estimates using travel receipts values that are reported by BEA and detailed counts of travelers by visa type from I-94 departure/arrivals records for 2009. For all countries, we have counts of business and leisure travelers who required a visa (B1, B2) or entered the United States under VWP. However, BEA officially reports travel receipts for only 33 countries and aggregated regions. We match the counts of travelers by travel purpose with travel receipts by aggregating counts for each region. Table C1 reports travel receipts and fractions of visa required and VWP business and leisure travelers from the matched data sets for the top twenty countries by travel receipts value.

Table C1 - Travel Receipts and Share of Travelers by Purpose of Visit Matched From BEA and I-94 Counts

Country/Region	Travel Receipts (in millions)	Business		Leisure	
		No Visa	Visa	No Visa	Visa
Japan	$9,495	7.33%	0.18%	64.63%	0.23%
United Kingdom	$8,884	11.15%	0.54%	85.63%	1.68%
Other South America	$7,082	0.01%	14.90%	0.21%	82.44%
Mexico	$5,991	0.00%	8.21%	0.05%	89.89%
Germany	$4,479	14.51%	0.60%	80.73%	1.37%
Other Europe	$3,868	7.96%	8.82%	49.48%	30.77%
Other Western Hemisphere	$3,331	1.12%	10.10%	2.64%	81.96%
Brazil	$3,318	0.01%	12.56%	0.30%	84.74%
France	$3,193	11.86%	0.55%	83.94%	1.35%
Australia	$2,974	12.74%	0.62%	83.58%	1.89%
China	$2,755	0.01%	30.55%	0.04%	47.54%
India	$2,577	0.01%	24.71%	0.02%	62.12%
Korea	$2,552	3.93%	11.72%	30.08%	28.93%
Italy	$2,190	10.99%	0.85%	84.43%	1.71%
Venezuela	$1,740	0.03%	10.33%	0.84%	86.53%
Spain	$1,596	8.46%	0.53%	87.44%	1.33%
Netherlands	$1,282	16.11%	0.51%	81.07%	0.99%
Other Africa	$1,225	0.04%	21.91%	0.56%	68.09%

Source: BEA and Author's Calculations.

We calculate the travel expenditures for each group of travelers by multiplying total travel receipts and shares of travelers by visa requirements. The caveat to this calculation is that it assumes that travel expenditures are equally distributed. In contrast, the SIAT data allow us to directly calculate the expenditure shares of travelers, because we observe expenditure value for each traveler. Table C2 reports the values of travel expenditure by travel purpose and visa type based on the population shares.

Table C2 - Total Expenditures Based on Population Shares of Visa-Required and Visa-Free Overseas Arrivals by Travel Type

33 Countries/Regions	Business		Leisure	
	No Visa	Visa	No Visa	Visa
Total	$4,830,722,622	$6,572,135,199	$33,677,873,026	$29,744,133,326
Shares	42 percent	58 percent	53 percent	47 percent
Visa share total	49 percent			

Source: Authors' calculations.

While total dollar value expenditures are slightly higher using BEA travel receipts, the expenditure shares of travelers by travel purpose and visa requirements are generally consistent with the respective expenditure shares we obtained using SIAT.[18] Specifically, the difference between the two estimates in shares of expenditure by leisure travelers who required a visa is less than one percent. We focus on the expenditure shares calculated from the SIAT data.

[18] BEA has internal methodology to adjust travel expenditures.

Appendix D. Population Weights in the SIAT Data

In the SIAT data, a responding traveler with a known country of citizenship is considered to be a "representative" traveler for that country. For example, if the population weight on a respondent from Brazil is 50, then that weight indicates that the respondent represents 50 travelers from Brazil with the same individual characteristics. By totaling all population weights, we can obtain the aggregate number of arrivals from any country.

To match the individual level data with an aggregate arrivals data by country of residence (I-94), CIC Research Inc. uses the following methodology to calculate the population weights:[19]

> The estimation of Non-Resident international air travel activity is a multi-step expansion process of the ITA-TI In-Flight Survey of International Air Travelers (IFS) data. There are a series of data preparation steps performed prior to initiating the expansion procedures outlined below. These initial steps take the raw data file through the creation of the working database, computer editing, and outlier analysis. A discussion of these steps will not be presented in this document.
>
> The primary activity for the expansion process is contained in several computer programs that are run in sequence. The Immigration and Naturalization Service (INS) Form I-94 data containing summarized port of entry by country of residence information is used as control totals during the expansion process of the International Air Travelers Non-Resident database. The I-94 data is received from the U.S. Department of Commerce on a quarterly basis.
>
> **Step 1: Initial Survey Expansion**
>
> This step accounts for the children traveling with each responding adult. The initial expansion factor is one, unless children are a part of the travel party. The composition of the travel party is taken from the IFS data. If children are present, the initial expansion factor has a value greater than one. The exact value of the factor is dependent on the number of children and adults in the party. The formula for the initial expansion factor can be expressed as follows:
>
> Initial expansion = 1 + (children count/adult count)

[19] The following steps are reprinted from "Description of Expansion Procedures for Estimating Non-Resident and Resident International Travel Activity", CIC Research, 1999

Step 2: I-94 Data Conversion

This step converts the codes in the I-94 data to compatible codes that have been predefined for the In-Flight Survey of International Air Travelers. The effected variables are the country of residence and port of entry.

Control totals from the I-94 data are generated at this time. The control total is a summation of the count of non-residents for each port by country of residence and is used throughout the expansion process.

Step 3: Summarize Survey Data

The IFS data using the country of residence and port of entry codes is summarized during this step. First, the I-94 data and the IFS are merged by country code and port of entry code. The resulting file contains the summarized counts from the I-94 data and the count of responses from the IFS, by country of residence and port of entry. The merged data is compared with the control total to ensure it matches.

Step 4: Divide In-Flight Survey of International Air Travelers Survey Data

Next, the file containing the summarized I-94 and IFS data is sorted, processed and divided into three different classifications.

1) Records that contain both the I-94 count, the Survey of International Air Travelers count, and country of residence and U.S. port of entry codes. (The majority of the data.)

2) Records that have missing country of residence or U.S. port of entry codes in the IFS data. (No match with the I-94 data.)

3) Records that hold I-94 data, for a country of residence and a U.S. port of entry but have no corresponding IFS data. (No match with the IFS data.)

Of the three record classifications identified, the last two types require further explanation.

Type two records do not have a matching pair of country of residence and port of entry codes with the I-94 data. Therefore, initial expansion generated for the number of adults and children is reset to zero so they will not be added into the control total.

The type three records are derived from the I-94 data and do not have any corresponding matches in the IFS data. A new "dummy" record is generated containing a final expansion factor, country of residence, and port of entry. This ensures the summation of the final expansion by country of residence and port of entry will equal the I-94 control total.

The total of the three sections will match the I-94 control total by country of residence and U.S. port of entry.

Step 5: Sort and Merge Data—Create Final Expansion

In this step, the Non-Resident file is read and sorted by the country of residence and port of entry.

The initial expansion values in the IFS file are summarized by country of residence and port of entry. This value will be used to proportion the I-94 expansion by the number of adults and children.

A respondent's final expansion value is created by taking the proportion of the respondent's initial expansion value to the sum of all initial expansion values (by country of residence and port of entry) multiplied by the I-94 totals by country of residence and port of entry. The calculation appears as follows:

final expansion = ((initial expansion/sum of initial expansion) * I-94 count)

The total of the final expansion value for all records in the Survey of International Air Travelers database will equal the I-94 control total.

Step 6: Create Comparison Table

The final step is run to check the I-94 table "Port of Entry by Country of Residence (Air Mode Only)" against the expanded estimate values in the IFS database. The results are shown in a cross tabulation table by world region and port of entry. The sum of the overseas visitors and the Mexican Air visitors from the IFS will equal the I-94 table control total.

Page intentionally left blank

www.ingramcontent.com/pod-product-compliance
Lightning Source LLC
Chambersburg PA
CBHW081819280526
45789CB00008B/3156
9781500319038